D0991789

Creating a City Park

Dividing Three-Digit Numbers by One-Digit Numbers Without Remainders

Frances E. Ruffin

PowerMath™

The Rosen Publishing Group's
PowerKids Press™
New York

Published in 2004 by The Rosen Publishing Group, Inc.
29 East 21st Street, New York, NY 10010

Book Design: Haley Wilson

Photo Credits: Cover © Gary Braasch/Corbis; p. 4 © Mug Shots/Corbis; pp. 7 (inset), 9 (inset), 13 (inset), 15 (inset), 17 (inset), 19 (inset) © PhotoDisc; p. 7 © Roger Spooner/Taxi; p. 9 © Richard Hutchings/Corbis; p. 11 (inset) © Spencer Jones/Taxi; p. 11 © Ariel Skelley/Corbis; p. 13 © C. Borland/Photolink/PhotoDisc; p. 15 © Darrell Gulin/Corbis; p. 17 © GoodShoot/SuperStock; p. 19 © Randy M. Ury/Corbis; p. 22 © SW Productions/Index Stock.

Library of Congress Cataloging-in-Publication Data

Ruffin, Frances E.
  Creating a city park : dividing three-digit numbers by one-digit numbers without remainders / Frances E. Ruffin.
       v. cm. — (PowerMath)
Includes index.
Contents: A garden in an empty lot — Splitting up the seeds — Dividing by subtracting — What's the quotient? — Finding the quotient — Tulips — A special entrance — Planting sunflowers — A party in the park — Dog division.
  ISBN 0-8239-8978-X (lib. bdg.)
  ISBN 0-8239-8926-7 (pbk.)
  6-pack ISBN: 0-8239-7454-5
  1. Division—Juvenile literature. 2. Mathematical recreations—Juvenile literature. [1. Division. 2. Parks.] I. Title. II. Series.
  QA115.R73 2004
  513.2'14—dc21

                              2003003805

Manufactured in the United States of America

Contents

Have you ever helped clean up your neighborhood?

A Garden in an Empty Lot

Some families who live in our apartment building wanted to create a city park in our neighborhood. We got a **permit** from the city's Parks Department to use the empty lot across the street for our park. To make the lot safe and clean, we **divided** up the work that had to be done. **Division** is a math operation we use in our lives every day. When we divide something, we break it up into equal parts.

Five of us helped clear the lot of leaves and trash. We had 100 bags to fill, and each person filled an equal number of bags. How many bags did each person fill?

$$
\begin{array}{r}
20 \\
5\overline{)100} \\
-10 \\
\hline
00
\end{array}
$$

Each person filled 20 bags.

Splitting Up the Seeds

We wanted our city park to have flowers, so we bought packs of wildflower seeds. Each pack of seeds would be divided into equal parts and planted in containers around the edges of the park. We had 180 containers and 6 packets of seeds. Before we planted the seeds, we needed to figure out how many containers would be planted with the seeds from each pack. Splitting up a group of things into many equal parts is a form of division.

The seeds in each seed pack would be divided up among 30 containers. That means that each seed packet would be divided into 30 equal parts.

6

The seed is the part of a plant that makes a new plant. Inside the seed is the young root and stem of the new plant, as well as stored food to help the new plant grow.

Dividing by Subtracting

Another way of dividing is to subtract the same number several times. Dave and his dad had 104 bushes to plant in the park. They wanted to plant the bushes in 8 equal rows. Dave and his dad took 8 bushes at a time—1 for each row—from the 104 bushes they had. Let's figure out how many bushes were in each row by using subtraction.

$$104 - 8 = 96$$
$$96 - 8 = 88$$
$$88 - 8 = 80$$
$$80 - 8 = 72$$
$$72 - 8 = 64$$
$$64 - 8 = 56$$
$$56 - 8 = 48$$
$$48 - 8 = 40$$
$$40 - 8 = 32$$
$$32 - 8 = 24$$
$$24 - 8 = 16$$
$$16 - 8 = 8$$
$$8 - 8 = 0$$

Now count how many times we subtracted 8 from 104 to get to zero. The answer is 13 times. That means there will be 13 bushes in each of the 8 rows.

We can show this as a division problem, too.

$$\begin{array}{r} 13 \\ 8\overline{)104} \\ -8 \\ \hline 24 \\ -24 \\ \hline 0 \end{array}$$

To plant each bush, Dave and his dad first dug a hole, then took a bush out of its pot and put it in the hole. Then they covered the roots with dirt and watered the bush.

What's the Quotient?

Jerry found a pile of 399 bricks in a corner of the lot. We decided to use the bricks to make 7 equal brick paths in our park. How many bricks would make up each of the 7 equal paths? We can divide 399 by 7 to get the answer. The **dividend** is the number to be divided: 399. The **divisor** is the number we divide by: 7. The **quotient** is the answer. What is the quotient?

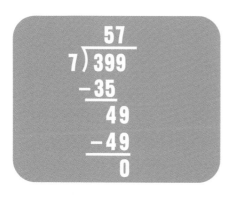

The quotient, or answer, is 57. That means that each path will be made of 57 bricks.

The first bricks were made about 8,000 years ago! Back then, people made bricks out of mud and clay and let them dry and harden in the sun.

Finding the Quotient

Julie and Tony decided they wanted to plant some **marigolds** in our city park. Marigolds produce an oil that keeps away small worms that eat the roots of plants. Julie and Tony went to the store and bought 176 marigolds. They planted the marigolds in 8 equal rows. How many marigolds were in each row? You can divide the dividend (176) by the divisor (8) to find the quotient.

The quotient is 22.
Each row would have
22 marigolds.

Julie and Tony told us that there are about 50 different kinds of marigolds. Marigolds can grow to be between 6 inches and 3 feet tall!

Tulips

We also planted tulips in our park. Tulips grow from bulbs that are planted in the ground. Their leaves, stems, and flowers grow from the bulb, and they can grow to be up to $2\frac{1}{2}$ feet tall.

We bought 115 tulip bulbs. We wanted to plant them in 5 equal rows. How many tulips would be in each row? We can divide the dividend (115) by the divisor (5) to find the quotient.

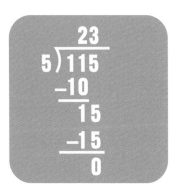

The quotient is 23.
Each row would have
23 tulips.

There are thousands of different kinds of tulips. Most of these developed from just a few kinds of tulips that were brought from Asia to Europe in the 1500s.

A Special Entrance

A plant **nursery** gave us 128 ivy plants for our garden. A few of us wanted to plant the ivy in the ground around the trees in the park. However, the **majority** of us wanted to plant the ivy in 8 large planters at the entrance to the park. We divided the ivy plants equally among the 8 planters. How many ivy plants did we put in each planter? You can divide the dividend (128) by the divisor (8) to find the quotient.

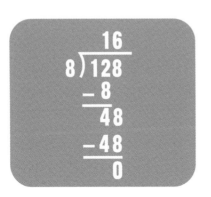

The quotient is 16.
Each planter would have
16 ivy plants.

We planted ground ivy, which was once used
to make medicine. We didn't want to use poison ivy,
which can hurt you if you touch it.

Planting Sunflowers

Mary's favorite flower is the sunflower, so she bought 207 sunflower seeds to plant. Sunflowers need lots of room to grow. They can grow to be 10 feet tall, and they can have blossoms that measure more than 1 foot across!

Mary decided to plant the sunflower seeds in 9 different areas of the park so they would have plenty of room to grow. She wanted to plant the same number of seeds in each area. To find out how many seeds she planted in each area, you can divide the dividend (207) by the divisor (9) to find the quotient.

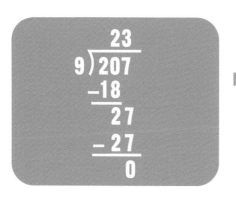

The quotient is 23. Mary planted 23 sunflower seeds in each area.

Did you know that 1 sunflower can produce about 1,000 seeds?

A Party in the Park

Finally it was time for our park to open. We decided to send notices to people in our neighborhood to invite them to our park opening party. Several of us **volunteered** to put the notices in mailboxes and to hand them out to people on the street.

We printed 750 notices and divided them equally among 5 volunteers. How many notices did each volunteer have to hand out? You can divide the dividend (750) by the divisor (5) to find the quotient.

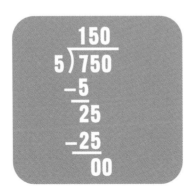

The quotient is 150.
Each of the 5 volunteers had
150 notices to hand out.

You are invited to the

Park Opening Party.

We have created

Marydale Park

for everyone to enjoy.

Come this Saturday
for fun in the park!

Pets are welcome!

Volunteering is a way to help out by giving up some
of your free time. We were able to create a beautiful city
park by volunteering just a little of our time!

Dog Division

The park opening party was a great success. Many of our neighbors brought their dogs. Mrs. Johnson had a large tin that held 104 dog treats. If she gave each dog that came to the park 2 dog treats, how many dogs could have treats? Divide the dividend (104) by the divisor (2) to find out.

$$\begin{array}{r} 52 \\ 2\overline{)104} \\ -10 \\ \hline 04 \\ -4 \\ \hline 0 \end{array}$$

52 dogs could have treats!

Glossary

divide (duh-VIDE) To break something into equal parts.

dividend (DIH-vuh-dehnd) A number that is divided by another number.

division (duh-VIH-zhun) The act of dividing one number by another number.

divisor (duh-VY-zur) A number by which another number is divided.

majority (muh-JOR-uh-tee) The larger number.

marigold (MAIR-uh-gold) A garden plant with yellow, orange, or red flowers.

nursery (NUR-suh-ree) A place where plants and trees are grown and sold.

permit (PUR-mit) A written order allowing someone to do something.

quotient (KWOH-shunt) The number you get by dividing one number by another number.

volunteer (vah-lun-TEER) To offer your time or services to help with something.

Index